Fantasy Chronicles

Fantastical Creatures and Magical Beasts

Shannon Knudsen

Lerner Publications Company · Minneapolis

Lerner Publications Company
A division of Lerner Publishing Group, Inc.
241 First Avenue North
Minneapolis, MN 55401 U.S.A.

Website address: www.lernerbooks.com

Library of Congress Cataloging-in-Publication Data

Knudsen, Shannon, 1971–
    Fantastical creatures and magical beasts / by Shannon Knudsen.
       p.   cm. — (Fantasy chronicles)
    Includes bibliographical references and index.
    ISBN-13: 978–0–8225–9987–6 (lib. bdg. : alk. paper)
    1. Animals, Mythical—Juvenile literature. I. Title.
  GR820.K58 2010
  398'.469—dc22   2009004794

Manufactured in the United States of America
2 – BP – 2/1/10

TABLE OF CONTENTS

CHAPTER 1

MEET THE MONSTERS

You hear feet thudding against the stone floor. It's the beast, on the prowl again. It grunts and snuffles as it lumbers through the maze, trying to catch a human scent.

Even though you're exhausted, fear sends a surge of energy through your body. You spring up from the shadowy corner where you'd been trying to steal a few minutes of rest. Time to look for a new hiding place.

You wonder how many of the others are still alive. Hours ago, King Minos locked fourteen of you inside this cursed maze, known as a labyrinth. Every year he requires the same sacrifice from the citizens of the Greek city of Athens: seven young women and seven young men. This unfortunate group must face death at the jaws of the Minotaur. This merciless half bull, half man wanders the maze. It is your unhappy fate to be among those sacrificed this year.

If only the labyrinth weren't so confusing! The passages twist and turn at such strange angles. You can't keep track of where you've been, much less where you're going. All you know is that you have to keep moving. Maybe there's a way out somewhere.

You round a corner, trying to move faster. A dead end! Quickly you turn around to run back to the intersection. And there it is.

The creature towers eight feet tall, and its horns almost touch the sides of the passageway. Its eyes glare at you, red and angry. There is nothing human about them.

It is the most terrifying thing you will ever see. It's also the last.

Scary and Imaginary

Have you ever felt so lucky that you didn't live in ancient Greece? Here's some good news: even if you had lived in Athens three thousand years ago, you wouldn't have been eaten by the Minotaur. It may sound like one terrifying beast, but it wasn't real. In fact, the creatures in this book do not really exist, and they never have. But that hasn't stopped people from telling stories about them for hundreds and even thousands of years.

Greek myths say that the Minotaur was the son
of Pasiphae, the wife of Minos, ruler of the island of
Crete, and of a snow-white bull. Minos was supposed to
sacrifce the bull to the gods, but he kept it.
A god punished him by making Pasiphae
fall in love with the bull.

What do these fantastic creatures have in common? What would you see if you could put ten of them together in a room? (It would have to be an awfully large room, by the way.) On the surface, they would probably look nothing alike. Some might be part human and part animal, like the Minotaur. Some might have wings, claws, or fangs. A couple might have all three. Some would breathe poison or fire or frost. Most of them would be pretty frightening. But one or two might turn out to be noble beasts once you got to know them.

No matter what they look like or what creepy powers they possess, these imaginary beings all exist for the same reasons. People tell stories about the things that scare them—the dark, the unknown, and the wild. For example, the Minotaur story describes people being trapped in a terrifying place, only to die a horrible death. Sometimes stories of fantastic beasts are also about overcoming our fears. The ancient Greeks probably never told the story of the Minotaur without including its very important ending. The hero Theseus was determined to help the people of Athens. So he volunteered to be sacrificed to the Minotaur. Theseus met the horned beast, faced him in combat, and killed him. How's that for a way to conquer what scares you?

This ancient Greek painting shows Theseus *(left)* slaying the Minotaur with a sword.

Most fantastical creatures weren't considered imaginary by the people who first told stories and wrote about them. Some, such as the Minotaur, came from the religious beliefs of ancient

cultures. Others were believed to be rare but real animals in the natural world. The phoenix fit into the second group. Many ancient Greek scholars wrote about this bright red and gold bird. It looked somewhat like an eagle. After living for several hundred years, the phoenix would burst into flame. Then it would be reborn from its ashes and start its life cycle again. Rather than scaring people, the phoenix comforted them. A bird that could defeat death helped people feel less afraid of dying themselves.

This phoenix appears in an English bestiary, or book of animals, from around 1200.

Another amazing beast that people believed to be real was the unicorn. Travelers who had been to India brought tales of this one-horned, horselike beast to ancient Greece. At first the Greeks thought unicorns were white, red, and black. Over time Europeans thought of unicorns as a solid white animal with a spiraling horn. The unicorn was pure of heart but fierce and solitary. There was only one way to capture it. If a young woman sat quietly in the forest where a unicorn lived, it would come to her and place its head in her lap.

Like the phoenix, the unicorn comforted people about their fears. A unicorn's horn could detect poison and cure its effects. This ability may not seem like a big deal. But in the days before people understood disease very well, they often thought that medical problems were caused by poison. If someone

This famous French tapestry from the 1400s shows a unicorn visiting a young woman in the forest.

thought his food or drink might be poisoned, he placed a piece of a unicorn's horn in his food or drink to detect the poison—that is, if he could afford a piece of a unicorn horn. People paid large sums of money for these so-called unicorn horns. Too bad all they got in return was the tusk of a rhino or some other completely normal animal.

Storms and Bones

Scientists and historians who study ancient cultures believe that people also made up fantastic creatures to explain parts of their world that they couldn't understand. A terrible hurricane or tsunami might have seemed less frightening if its victims knew what caused it. How about a sea monster wriggling under the ocean, for example?

In the country of Zambia in southern Africa, people told traditional stories about creatures called lightning monsters. These creepy crawlers had the front body, legs, and head of a goat. And they had the back legs and tail of a crocodile. Lightning monsters spent most of their time in the heavens. But during a storm, they bounced down to the earth on threads. When they bounced back to the skies, they created lightning. If a lightning monster's thread broke, however, the monster had be found and killed by a warrior. Otherwise, the lightning monster would destroy the land.

The story about lightning monsters explained how lightning was created. And it did something else. It reassured the people in

Zambia that the lightning would end after the monsters returned to the heavens. Of course, the threat of the breaking thread sounded even scarier than a lightning storm. Maybe that gave the people who heard this story something else to think about during the storm!

Water Monsters

Every culture has stories of mysterious creatures that live in oceans, lakes, rivers, or streams. Some help us to express our fear of storms, shipwrecks, and drowning. Others just make wonderfully scary tales. Famous sea monsters include the long-necked Loch Ness Monster of Scotland. (Its nickname is Nessie.) A legendary Scandinavian giant squid, the Kraken, is big enough to crush a ship with its tentacles. And then there's the kelpie, a Celtic water horse with supernatural powers. It lures victims into a river, drowns them, and consumes them.

Fantastic creatures have also entered our stories as a result of fossil discoveries. The griffin is one example. This beast had the body and tail of a lion and the front legs and head of an eagle. It also had a pair of large ears. Ancient Greek writers described griffins living in eastern Asia. There they guarded huge treasures of gold and tore to pieces anyone who tried to steal the gold.

This golden griffin pendant comes from the ancient Greek city of Mycenae.

During the 1990s, a scholar named Adrienne Mayor noticed something interesting about the fossils of *Protoceratops*, a dinosaur found in eastern Asia. The dinosaur's beaklike jaw, long tail, and other features looked very much like ancient Greek descriptions of a griffin! Many scholars agree that these fossils probably inspired tales of the griffin. Travelers from eastern Asia brought stories about the griffin to Greece.

This painting shows an artist's idea of what *Protoceratops* might have looked like.

It's no coincidence that those ancient Greeks keep coming up, by the way. The more you learn about fabulous beasts, the more you'll see that the Greeks told some of the best monster stories in human history. Let's take a closer look at a few of their biggest stars.

CHAPTER 2

THE BEASTS OF ANCIENT GREECE

The civilization of the ancient Greeks began in about 1100 B.C. and lasted until 146 B.C. Fantastical creatures and magical animals played a big role in ancient Greece, especially in religion and storytelling.

The Greeks believed that monsters were part of a very real and dangerous world of gods, heroes, and magic. A few monsters were helpful to humans. But most of these fantastical creatures posed a threat. Some, such as the Minotaur, cared only about their own desires and appetites. Others worked for the gods.

The Harpies belonged to this second group. These giant birds had the head of a woman, powerful claws, and a rotten temper. Their name means "snatcher." They did the most snatching for Zeus, ruler of the gods. Zeus had his good side. But he could be petty and cruel at times. He became angry at Phineas, a man who had the gift of telling the future. Phineas gave away too many of the gods' plans, Zeus thought. So Zeus condemned him to live forever on an island with a buffet of delicious food. Every time Phineas began to eat, the Harpies swooped down from the sky and stole the tasty morsels from his hands. Harpies also had a reputation for kidnapping and tormenting travelers.

Medusa's Hissing Hair

Another famously nasty monster was Medusa. She began her life as a woman, not a beast. But then she angered the goddess Athena. That's never a good idea! Athena turned Medusa into a monster called a gorgon. She changed Medusa's long hair into a mass of squirming, hissing snakes. Athena made Medusa's pretty face so hideous that anyone who looked at it would turn into stone.

Medusa ran away from her home. Wherever she went, she left behind stone statues of the unfortunate people who saw her face. At last she took refuge in a cave with two other gorgons. By then, people hated her throughout the land for all the deaths she had caused. Soon the cave filled with the stone statues of still more men

In some versions of Medusa's story, the three gorgons are sisters. The other two are named Stheno and Euryale. Their parents were an ancient god and a sea monster.

who had tried to kill her. No one could attack her without looking at her. So in every case, the warrior turned to stone, while Medusa survived unharmed.

Then along came Perseus. A king charged this bold young man with the task of slaying the gorgon. Perseus had help in his mission from Medusa's old enemy, Athena. She told Perseus not to gaze upon Medusa directly. Instead, he should keep his back to her and hold up his shield so that he could see her reflection in its shiny surface.

Perseus wisely took the goddess's advice when he reached the gorgon's hideout. Studying the reflection in his shield, he found Medusa asleep. He cut off her head. Then he carefully placed it in a sack, which he took with him. On his journey home, he used the head against several enemies. He pulled it out of the sack without warning. When they saw it, they turned to stone. Later, he gave the head to Athena. She attached it to her shield to use in the same way.

A Three-Headed Monster

Medusa's power lived on in other ways too. When Perseus killed her, a white horse with gold wings sprang from her blood. Its name was Pegasus, from a Greek word meaning "strong." The horse lived up to that description. He was far too powerful to be tamed in any ordinary way. Pegasus knew that no bridle made by humans could hold him. He lived wild and free until Athena again became part

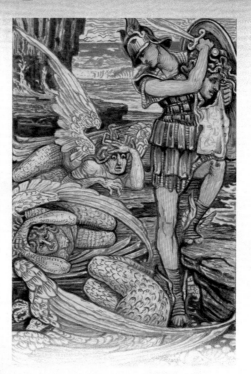

Two gorgons hide as Perseus puts Medusa's head in a sack. This picture comes from an 1892 painting by British artist Walter Crane.

of the tale. She wanted to help another young hero, Bellerophon, complete a difficult task. So she gave him a magical golden bridle and told him where to find Pegasus. Bellerophon threw the bridle on Pegasus, and the horse was tamed. Pegasus became a loyal and trustworthy steed.

With the speed and agility of his horse to aid him, Bellerophon set out to destroy another famous monster of Greek mythology. This nasty fire-breather was known as the Chimera. It had three heads: a lion's, a goat's, and a serpent's. Its body was made up of parts of all three animals. And the Chimera breathed fire. So no fighter could approach close enough to strike the monster. Not until Bellerophon, that is.

Mounted on Pegasus, Bellerophon could dart in and out of the range of the Chimera's flaming breath, firing arrows. Next, he took a spear that had a lump of lead welded to one end. The Chimera's breath melted the lead as Bellerophon thrust the spear into one of its evil mouths. The molten metal destroyed the creature as Bellerophon and Pegasus flew safely out of reach.

Bellerophon and Pegasus (right) face the Chimera on this painted Greek vase from the 500s B.C.

Fantastical Horses

The unicorn and Pegasus are probably the most famous mythical horses around. But they aren't the only ones. The Norse myths of Scandinavia include stories about a horse called Sleipnir (*below*), for example. Sleipnir carried Odin, ruler of the Norse gods, from the land of the gods to the land of men. Sleipnir means "smooth" or "gliding." The horse traveled equally well through air and on land, thanks to his eight strong legs.

A dappled (spotted) horse called Sharatz belonged to King Marko of Serbia. (Marko was a real person. But he has become the subject of many legends that include magic and incredible deeds.) Sharatz could fly fast enough to catch a fairy. He could leap the length of four lances, or spears. And he could jump as high as three lances too. When his hooves struck the earth, cracks appeared and sparks flew. Blue flame leaped from his nostrils. In battle, Sharatz trampled enemy soldiers. He also bit the ears off their horses.

All in the Family

The Chimera had several monstrous siblings that starred in stories of their own. The Hydra was an enormous serpent. It lived in the swamps of a part of southern Greece called Lerna. This monster had nine heads. If you cut off one of them, two would grow back in its place. Even worse, one of the nine heads couldn't be destroyed by any weapon. And each head's breath smelled so nasty that the slightest whiff would kill a person.

All these traits must have made the Hydra impossible to kill, right? That's what the people of Lerna believed. Whenever the Hydra left its swampy home, it lay waste to the land, destroying homes and cattle. No one could figure out how to stop it.

Along came yet another brave hero, Hercules. He had a sad history. In a fit of insanity, he had killed his wife and children. Hercules was determined to prove how sorry he was. He asked for advice from a priestess of the god Apollo. She told him to serve a man named Eurystheus for twelve years. Hercules would have to do anything he asked.

Eurystheus turned out to be a cruel master. He chose the most impossible tasks he could think of so that Hercules would fail. One of these tasks was to kill the Hydra of Lerna.

Dutifully, Hercules set off for southern Greece with his nephew, Iolaus. They tracked the Hydra to its marshy lair (hideout). Hercules attacked it with his enormous club. Sure enough, each time he clubbed off one of the Hydra's venom-breathing heads, two more took its place. The battle looked hopeless.

Then Iolaus had an inspiration. He set a torch on fire. As Hercules clubbed off another head of the Hydra, Iolaus used the torch to burn the headless stump. The fire sealed the stump, and nothing grew back! Soon only the last head remained—the one that a weapon could not destroy. Hercules clubbed it off the Hydra's body, but the head remained alive. So Hercules buried it under a boulder. At last, the Hydra was no more. Hercules dipped his arrows in the monster's poison to make them fatal to anyone he shot.

Hercules spent many years on a series of other labors that Eurystheus asked him to perform. Finally, Eurystheus sent him to face another sibling of the Chimera and the Hydra. This beast was a dog called Cerberus. It had

Hercules burns the Hydra's last head before crushing it with a boulder.

three heads, a mane of living snakes, and a huge snake's tail. One of his heads could see the past, while another saw the present. The third head could look ahead through time into the future. Cerberus served as the watchdog of Hades, who ruled the land of the dead. The monster dog stood guard at the gates of the Underworld. It allowed the spirits of the dead to enter—but never to leave.

Cerberus was said to be the son of a fire-breathing giant and Echidna, a woman who was half woman and half snake. Cerberus also had a brother, Orthrus, a dog with two heads. Hercules killed Orthrus while meeting one of Eurystheus's challenges.

The clever Eurystheus didn't charge Hercules with killing the demon dog. That would have been hard enough. Instead, Hercules had to capture Cerberus alive and bring him back to Eurystheus—without using weapons! Fortunately for Hercules, his years of heroic labors had attracted the favor of the gods. The goddess Athena and Hermes, the messenger of the gods, helped him enter the Underworld safely.

Soon Hercules found himself face-to-face with the snarling three-headed beast. Hercules wrestled Cerberus to the ground and

This vase, painted around 525 B.C. in Italy, shows Hercules delivering Cerberus to Eurystheus, who is hiding in a vase.

quieted him. It was a feat of strength that only he could have managed. He slung the dog over his shoulder and carried him all the way back to Eurystheus. As for Eurystheus, he was so frightened of the hound of Hades that he leaped into a tall vase to hide! He agreed to free Hercules forever if the hero would take Cerberus straight back to the Underworld. Of course, Hercules accepted the deal.

The list of fantastical Greek creatures goes on far beyond those you've met so far. In fact, some historians spend their entire lives studying the myths of ancient Greece. But the rest of the world has plenty of beasts to offer as well.

CHAPTER 3

Beasts Around the World

The ancient kingdom of Persia included the land we know as Iran. Persia gave rise to a culture as complex as that of the ancient Greeks. And it existed during about the same time period. The Persians told stories about a terrible beast called the manticore. Its name means "man-eater." The manticore had the body of a red lion but the face and ears of a man— except for its extra-wide mouth and three rows of super sharp teeth. Its long, flexible tail was topped with poisonous quills. The manticore could shoot them at enemies either behind it or ahead of it. As if that weren't enough, some descriptions of this nasty animal included front claws like a badger's. They were perfect for digging tunnels.

Travelers spread the news of the Persian manticore to the ancient Greeks. To the Greeks, this was no mythical beast. People claimed to have actually encountered it. So surely it was real. Greek scholars wrote long, frightening descriptions of the manticore. As these writings were read and repeated, more people came to believe in the man-eating beast.

This 1579 drawing of a basilisk shows a crown-shaped crest on the snake's head. The crown caused the basilisk to be called the king of serpents.

The same thing happened with another Persian creature, the desert-dwelling basilisk. This yellow snake sounded harmless enough at first. It was only a couple of feet long, had no dangerous spines, and did not breathe fire. But the basilisk didn't need fancy weapons. It had the power to strike dead anyone who so much as looked at or touched it. Just in case those defenses didn't work, the basilisk's breath could wither plants, animals, and people. If you managed to strike one with a weapon without looking at it, touching it, or breathing in its poison, you were still doomed. The basilisk's powerful venom would travel along your weapon and kill you!

No one seemed to ask one important question about basilisks. If no one could look at one without dying, how did anyone know for sure what basilisks looked like—or even whether they existed at all?

Perhaps this small, sneaky snake frightened people so much that the question just never crossed anyone's mind. Or maybe everyone was too busy worrying about how to survive a basilisk attack. Some stories said that only a weasel could kill a basilisk. Others recommended the crow of a rooster. Desert travelers in the Middle East and Africa began to carry one animal or the other. Sometimes they carried both, just in case. Otherwise, the only hope of defeating a basilisk was to cover yourself with mirrors to trick the beast into looking at its reflection. If a basilisk saw itself, even in a reflection, it would die.

Nobody agreed on what a basilisk looked like. German artist Albrecht Durer drew a basilisk with a serpent's tail and a rooster's body around 1512.

African Monsters

In southern Africa, a traditional tale of the Khoikhoi people warns of the dangerous Hai-uri. This beast is exactly half human—and he has no other half at all! The Hai-uri has half of a man's body and head, including one eye, half a nose and mouth, one arm, and one leg. His leg is so strong and fast that the Hai-uri can leap over patches of brush and rough ground. That ability comes in handy when he chases after his favorite meal—human beings. As ugly as the Hai-uri is, he doesn't have to hunt alone. The Bi-blouk is just like him, but she is female.

An extraordinary beast of western Africa is Aido Hwedo, an enormous snake who helped create the world. Aido Hwedo carried the god Mawu through the universe as Mawu made the stars and planets. To keep up his energy on the long journey, Aido Hwedo ate large amounts of iron. As a result, every morning he pooped enormous mounds on the planets Mawu made! The mounds became mountains.

> Western African stories say that Aido Hwedo didn't like the heat. So Mawu created the oceans beneath the continents so that the snake would stay cool.

As the earth grew, Mawu realized that it was getting too heavy. He gave Aido Hwedo a new job. The snake was to coil himself beneath the continents and hold them up. This difficult task sometimes makes the snake tremble with pain. Whenever he does, an earthquake occurs. What will happen when Earth runs out of iron for Aido Hwedo to eat? He'll stop holding up the continents, and they'll sink into the ocean.

Terrifying Creatures from Australia and Asia

The story of Aido Hwedo is one of many snake myths that have been passed from one generation to the next in cultures all over the world. Several of the native peoples of Australia tell of rainbow serpents. These snakes created Earth's river-beds and streams as they crawled across the land. During normal rain-fall, rainbow serpents rise into the sky, where they shine as rainbows. In dry weather, the snakes sleep bur-

An Australian Aboriginal artist of the twentieth century made this painting of a rainbow serpent.

rowed under mud. But if their sleep is disturbed, they may cause sudden flooding so deep that it can destroy a whole community.

A much scarier Australian creature is the Namorodo of Arnhem Land, in the northern part of the continent. The native peoples of this area describe the Namorodo as having a skeleton like a human's. But it has no skin, blood, muscles, or veins. Strands of tissue called ligaments hold the bones together. The Namorodo looks very creepy indeed. It has no stomach, but it still gets hungry. It prefers to drink human blood, which it drains from sleeping people at night.

Asia has plenty of terrifying monsters too. A famous and fantastical beast of China is Xiang Liu. It is a servant of the evil dragon Gong Gong. Xiang Liu had the body of a huge, black snake. Its nine heads had human faces. He was so big that each of the nine heads fed from a different mountain, all at the same time. As Xiang Liu slithered across the land, his body transformed it into a smelly, disgusting marsh where no animals or people could survive.

Not all giant snakes are bad news. In some Asian countries, giant snakes called *nagas* protect places sacred to the Buddhist faith. A many-headed cobra naga sometimes forms the throne on which the Buddha, founder of Buddhism, sits, as we can see in sculptures like the one below.

Bestiary Wisdom: Dragons

Some stories about Aido Hwedo describe him as a dragon, rather than as a serpent. Practically every culture in the world has legends about massive reptiles, often with wings. Dragons are especially important in the mythology of China, for example. In many stories, dragons display incredible intelligence. They often guard important treasures and secrets too.

This Chinese dragon appears on a wall in Beijing.

One of the greatest heroes of China, Yu, finally killed Xiang Liu. But the serpent's blood poisoned the ground so badly that grain would not grow there. (This story is a myth, but Yu was a real person.)

The *baku* of Japan may look frightening, but its behavior is rather friendly. In traditional artwork from the 1700s, the baku has horns and a tiger's claws. But it has the head, tusks, and trunk of an elephant. This bizarre beast actually helps people by feeding on their nightmares. After the baku has had its meal, the dreamer returns to a peaceful sleep. One way to encourage the baku to eat your bad dreams is to keep a picture of it in your bedroom. Another

After many heroic adventures, Yu became emperor of China. He was known as Yu the Great.

is to carry a small statue of the creature with you. If a nightmare wakes you up anyhow, just call for help. Say, "Devour, oh baku!" You'll be back to sleep in no time.

American Beasts

The traditional stories of the Seneca people include the tale of a monstrous creature called Ganiagwaihegowa. (The Seneca are Native Americans who live mainly in the northeastern United States.) The monster looked like a massive bear, but it had no fur. This creature was known not just for its size but also for its habit of eating bears. It ate people too. Ganiagwaihegowa lived in the Underworld and crept forth to hunt at night.

Two Seneca men, Hadentheni and Hanigongendatha, wanted to save their people from Ganiagwaihegowa. They asked a spirit for information. According to the spirit, the evil monster's only weakness was in the bottoms of its front feet. The men traveled to the Underworld and found the monster's lair. During the long fight that followed, Ganiagwaihegowa reared up on its hind legs. The warriors quickly shot the soles of his front feet, and the beast fell to the ground, dead. The men cut off his feet and burned the body to make sure that he would never terrorize the Seneca again.

Far to the south, the Quechua people of the Andes Mountains of South America tell of a catlike monster. The monster creates brutal storms that often destroy crops in this part of the world. Known as the Ccoa, this gray, striped beast has a large head and eyes that glow like fire. When angry, the Ccoa flies through the air spitting balls of ice from its mouth. Lightning jumps from its eyes. For centuries the Quechua have made offerings of incense and llama fat to Ccoa to prevent these storms.

CHAPTER 4

Beasts Still Scare Us

Fantastical creatures continue to enchant people all over the globe. We still tell the old stories of ancient mythology. And we continue to imagine new beasts that are stranger and scarier than any the world has seen. Our books, movies, and games show our fascination with these bizarre creatures.

Author Lewis Carroll included both old and new creatures in his world-famous children's book *Alice's Adventures in Wonderland*. (Many people simply call it *Alice in Wonderland*.) Published in 1865, *Alice* features a griffin. The story also features many talking animals. One of them, the Cheshire Cat, likes to vanish completely, except for its toothy smile.

A new kind of creature became one of the scariest characters in L. Frank Baum's children's book, *The Wizard of Oz*. Baum introduced the world to winged monkeys in 1900, when Dorothy's adventures were first published. But it was the 1939 movie that made the monkeys famous. Viewers had never seen such a frightening portrayal of a fantastical creature. People who grew up watching *The Wizard of Oz* still mention winged monkeys when they want to describe something especially creepy!

Another famous movie of the 1930s introduced the giant ape King Kong. In the film *King Kong*, the ape lives on a tropical island with dinosaurs and other unusual creatures. He is captured and taken to New York City, where he escapes. Kong is so large that he can climb the Empire State Building. But he is killed by gunfire from airplanes. This enormous ape made such an impression on audiences that the movie spawned several sequels and remakes. Most recently, the 2005 film *King Kong* brought the tale to modern viewers.

C. S. Lewis's *The Chronicles of Narnia* appeared more than fifty years ago. They have been widely read ever since. The seven-book series has been made into several movies, starring many talking animals and other fantastical beasts. In the land of Narnia, unicorns, winged horses, and a purple-tailed phoenix support Aslan, the talking lion. Aslan fights the forces of the evil White Witch, while Minotaurs take her side.

The popular author Rick Riordan has based an entire series on the gods, goddesses, and beasts of Greek mythology. Percy Jackson and the Olympians

In this 1930 poster for the movie *King Kong*, the giant ape stands on top of the Empire State Building.

tells the story of a modern boy who discovers he is a son of Poseidon, god of the sea. Percy's adventures in the first book, *The Lightning Thief*, include a Minotaur, the head of Medusa, and wise old Chiron, who is a centaur (half man and half horse). Another Percy Jackson book, *The Titan's Curse*, features a manticore as the headmaster of a military school. *The Lightning Thief* is being made into a movie, so many of these creatures will be visiting a theater near you!

If you've read the Harry Potter series, you surely recognized many of the monsters mentioned in this book. Author J. K. Rowling drew on many myths and ancient stories to populate Harry's world with these creatures. She often changed them in small ways to fit her stories. Fawkes the phoenix has the ability to be reborn after dying in a burst of flame, for example. But his tears have a special, secret power that Rowling invented herself.

Fawkes the phoenix appears on the cover of the British edition of *Harry Potter and the Order of the Phoenix*, the fifth book in the series.

Fantastical Play

Games give us a chance to imagine battling monsters and magical animals or even making friends with them. Some of the oldest arcade games took their inspiration from fantastical beasts. For example, the 1980 arcade game called *Phoenix* challenged the player to destroy alien birds. Players eventually face a brightly colored, bird-shaped mothership. (This ship was the first boss ever in an arcade game!) After defeating the mothership, the player faced another round of challenges at a greater difficulty level. If the player succeeded, he or she encountered the mothership again. The mothership's reappearance was like the rebirth of the ancient phoenix.

Plenty of modern video games also make use of magical creatures. Many games are based on the Harry Potter series, *King Kong*, and *The Chronicles of Narnia*. In game series such as *Final Fantasy*, *EverQuest*, and *World of Warcraft*, you'll find monsters inspired by Hydras, Minotaurs, gorgons, and unicorns.

This statue shows one of the Minotaur-like Tauren characters from *World of Warcraft*.

Gargoyles

The gargoyle (below) is a type of monster that began its life not in stories but upon buildings. The first gargoyles appeared as stone carvings at the edges of rooftops during the Middle Ages (A.D. 500–1500). They had open mouths, which channeled rainwater off the roof. These gargoyles often looked like people. But many were a combination of a person and an animal. Over time, gargoyles became more and more monstrous. They also began to appear on buildings as decorations, not just to funnel water to the ground.

The gargoyle has since entered modern books and games as a monster with sharp claws, fangs, and wings. It appears in fantasy stories and in the role-playing game *Dungeons & Dragons*. *D & D* also features a type of sea-dwelling gargoyle called the kapoacinth.

Two boys show off their recent Pokémon game card purchases in New York City.

The *Monster Rancher* series of video games was first launched in 1997. It allows players to create and raise their own creatures. The creatures then go to battle in tournaments. Another series, *Spore*, extends that idea. Players not only create their own fantastical beasts but also guide them as they evolve into civilizations. The civilizations become so advanced that the beasts travel to outer space.

Trading-card games borrow from ancient mythology as well. *Magic: The Gathering* features centaurs, for example. Two extremely popular card games from Japan include creatures inspired by the dream-eating baku. The Bakumon of the game

Digimon consumes nightmares. In *Pokémon* the Drowzee has the power to put people to sleep and detect what they are dreaming. Then it decides which dreams to eat.

From books to movies to games, fabulous creatures will always be part of our culture. They continue to fascinate us, frighten us, and make our world a more interesting place, just as they have for thousands of years. Best of all, a new creature is no farther away than your imagination. The next time you're bored, see what kind of story you can add to our many tales of fantastical animals and magical beasts.

Selected Bibliography

Clair, Colin. *Unnatural History: An Illustrated Bestiary*. New York: Abelard-Schuman, 1967.

Dale-Green, Patricia. *Lore of the Dog*. Boston: Houghton Mifflin Company, 1967.

Gilmore, David D. *Monsters: Evil Beings, Mythical Beasts, and All Manner of Imaginary Terrors*. Philadelphia: University of Pennsylvania Press, 2003.

Howey, M. Oldfield. *The Horse in Magic and Myth*. London: William Rider & Son, 1923.

Lum, Peter. *Fabulous Beasts*. London: Thames and Hudson, 1952.

Mayor, Adrienne. *The First Fossil Hunters: Paleontology in Greek and Roman Times*. Princeton, NJ: Princeton University Press, 2000.

Morford, Mark P. O., and Robert J. Lenardon. *Classical Mythology*. 5th ed. White Plains, NY: Longman Publishers, 1995.

Rose, Carol. *Giants, Monsters, and Dragons*. New York: W. W. Norton & Company, 2001.

Rose, H. J. *A Handbook of Greek Mythology*. New York: Dutton & Co., 1959.

Sax, Boria. *The Mythical Zoo: An Encyclopedia of Animals in World Myth, Legend, and Literature*. Santa Barbara, CA: ABC-CLIO, 2001.

Wilson, David John. *Indigenous South Americans of the Past and Present*. Boulder, CO: Westview Press, 1999.

Yang, Lihui, and An Deming. *Handbook of Chinese Mythology.* Santa Barbara, CA: ABC-CLIO, 2005.

Further Reading and Websites
Books

Krensky, Stephen. *Creatures from the Deep.* Minneapolis: Lerner Publications Company, 2007. This book from the Monster Chronicles series introduces water-dwelling beasts from all over the world. The Ancient Greeks told of the evil Scylla and Charybdis, who destroyed ships and ate sailors. And in India, a legendary fish called the Makara had the head of an elephant. From sea monsters to the giant whale Moby Dick, Krensky looks at how creatures from the deep have captured our imaginations in myths, folktales, and popular culture.

————. *Dragons.* Minneapolis: Lerner Publications Company, 2007. Another book in the Monster Chronicles series features dragons from throughout history. Krensky explains that people from many cultures have told stories about dragons for more than five thousand years. In ancient China, people believed that emperors were descended from dragons. The Vikings admired dragons so much that they carved dragon heads at the front of their ships. And in modern culture, the dragon is such a popular beast that it stars in its own films, books, and games.

Rowling, J. K. *Fantastic Beasts and Where to Find Them.* New York: Scholastic Press, 2001. Rowling penned this book under the name of Newt Scamander. He's a magizoologist, Rowling's word for a scientist who studies magical animals. Newt Scamander is also the author of the textbook that Harry Potter studies during his first year at Hogwarts. This volume is that very book, an A-to-Z listing of the incredible creatures that live in Harry's world. And since it's Harry's own copy, it includes the notes he wrote on many entries.

Storrie, Paul. *Hercules: The Twelve Labors: A Greek Myth*. Illustrated by Steve Kurth. Minneapolis: Graphic Universe, 2007. The myth of the labors of Hercules is retold in this full-color graphic novel. The Greek hero battles several fantastical beasts and survives other adventures to free himself from service to Eurystheus. This book is part of the Graphic Myths and Legends series, which also includes volumes about Perseus and Medusa as well as Yu and the dragon Gong Gong.

Websites

Ancient Greece for Kids: Mythology
http://greece.mrdonn.org/myths.html
This website includes descriptions of Greek gods and retells many myths. The stories of the Minotaur, Medusa, and Hercules are here. Viewers can also follow links to learn more about the culture of ancient Greece.

Percy Jackson and the Olympians
http://www.percyjacksonbooks.com/
The official website of the popular book series by Rick Riordan

offers plenty of information for fans. Visitors can read the first chapter of each book online, download games related to the series, and solve puzzles. There's also a page for each Olympian, god, and monster, featuring artwork, hometowns, and weapons of choice.

World Myths and Legends in Art
http://www.artsmia.org/world-myths/artbytheme/animalmyths.html
The Minneapolis Institute of Arts presents photos and descriptions of artwork with animals and beasts from the world's myths. Carvings, sculpture, and ceremonial clothing reveal how fantastical beasts have their place in stories from all over the globe. The examples include Navajo, Greek, Nigerian, and Melanesian tales. Background information about each culture is included as well.

Movies and TV

The Chronicles of Narnia: The Lion, the Witch, and the Wardrobe. DVD. Burbank, CA: Walt Disney Pictures, 2005. When the Pevensie children move to a new home, Lucy discovers a magical wardrobe that contains a portal to a different world. In Narnia, the White Witch has control, and winter has covered the land for one hundred years. The Pevensies must help the good lion Aslan and his army of helpful beasts to defeat the White Witch and save Narnia from evil. The second film in the Narnia series, The Chronicles of Narnia: Prince Caspian, was released in 2008.

King Kong. DVD. Los Angeles: Universal Studios, 2005. Peter
   Jackson, director of the *Lord of the Rings* trilogy, remade the
   famous 1933 film for modern viewers. Skull Island is home to
   bizarre dinosaurs, giant spiders, and the gigantic ape King Kong.
   The capture of Kong leads to a showdown in New York City
   in which the ape climbs the Empire State Building and battles
   aircraft. This film won three Academy Awards for its incredible
   visual effects and sound.

The Wizard of Oz. DVD. Burbank, CA: Warner Home Video, 2002.
   This 1939 musical brought the children's book by L. Frank
   Baum to the movies. A girl named Dorothy is struck unconscious
   during a tornado at her home in Kansas. She awakens in the
   magical Land of Oz and must find her way home. Several
   fantastical friends help her, including the Tin Man, the
   Scarecrow, and the Cowardly Lion, who are all partly human.
   The winged monkeys of the Wicked Witch of the West pursue
   the group as they make their way.

Index

About the Author

Shannon Knudsen has written books for young readers about elephants, mayors, the explorer Leif Eriksson, the reporter Nellie Bly, and many other topics. She lives with her cat and her dog in Tucson, Arizona. When she isn't writing, she likes to explore the desert and see how many of its plants and animals she can name.

Photo Acknowledgments

The images in this book are used with the permission of: © Fortean Picture Library, pp. 1, 7, 11; The Art Archive/Bodleian Library Oxford, p. 8; © French School/The Bridgeman Art Library/Getty Images, p. 9; The Art Archive/National Archaeological Museum Athens/ Gianni Dagli Orti, p. 12; © DEA Picture Library/De Agostini Picture Library/Getty Images, p. 13; Picture Collection, The Branch Libraries, The New York Public Library, Astor, Lenox and Tilden Foundations, p. 17; © Erich Lessing/Art Resource, NY, pp. 18, 27, 30; The Art Archive/Historiska Muséet Stockholm/Alfredo Dagli Orti, p. 19; © Stefano Bianchetti/CORBIS, p. 21; © Réunion des Musées Nationaux/Art Resource, NY, p. 23; © Mary Evans Picture Library/The Image Works, p. 26; © age fotostock/SuperStock, p. 29; © JTB Photo Communications, Inc./Alamy, p. 31; Sandy Carruthers, © 2007 by Lerner Publishing Group, p. 32; © Buyenlarge/Time & Life Pictures/Getty Images, p. 36; © Pascal Le Segretain/Getty Images, p. 37; © Cindy Yamanaka/The Orange County Register/ZUMA Press, p. 38; © Geoff Manasse/Stockbyte/Getty Images, p. 39; © Evan Agostini/Getty Images, p. 40. © Bill Hauser/Independent Picture Service, pp. 4, 14-15, 24, 34. All page backgrounds illustrated by © Bill Hauser/Independent Picture Service.

Front Cover: © Mauricio Herrera/el-grimlock.deviantart.com.